Hopes Fulfilled

The Irish Immigrants in Boston

Table of Contents

Introduction

The United States is sometimes called a melting pot. Do you know why?

A melting pot is a place where many different people live. Throughout history, many different groups of people have come to the United States. They have brought with them their own cultures and traditions. Over time, these traditions have melted together with those of other people to form a strong, diverse country.

People who leave their country to live somewhere else are called **immigrants**. Many immigrants have come to the United States. They believe in the promise of America. They believe that they can have a good life here.

One group of immigrants came from Ireland. Many Irish immigrants settled in the city of Boston, Massachusetts. They had many challenges, or conflicts, to face. This story tells how they solved those conflicts.

Immigrant families leaving Ireland

Who Are Immigrants?

Most people love their country. Their friends and family are nearby. They enjoy the customs and traditions that make their country special. They are proud to speak the language and tell people where they live.

So why would people decide to leave their country forever? It is not an easy choice to make. Two things cause people to leave. They are called the "push" and "pull" factors.

The "push" is something that pushes people away from their country. Maybe a war has started or jobs are hard to find. People feel "pushed" out of their country.

Then there is the "pull." This is when another country pulls people toward it. The United States is sometimes that country. Many people believe in America's promises. America promises that if people work hard, they can have a nice life. The people don't want to leave their country, but they may feel that they have no choice—to America they must go! They have become immigrants.

About 150 years ago, many Irish people became immigrants. At that time, Ireland was ruled by England. Most of the land in Ireland was owned by English people. The English people allowed the Irish farmers to live on the land, but the land wasn't free. The Irish farmers had to pay **rent** to the English owners. They did not pay the rent with money, but with food. Most of the crops they planted had to be given to the English. The only crop the Irish could keep was potatoes.

Then in 1845, something terrible happened. The potato crop was rotten, and all of the potatoes turned black. People were starving— and dying. This era in Irish history is called the Potato **Famine**. England offered some help, but it was not enough. Many Irish families felt forced to leave Ireland. The lack of food pushed them out.

But the promises of the United States pulled them toward America's shores.

Families struggled during the Potato Famine.

If leaving Ireland was hard, then the trip to America may have been even harder.

First, the Irish family had to have enough money. Such a long journey was expensive.

Then they had the trip across the Atlantic Ocean. At that time, planes had not been invented, so people traveled across the ocean by boat. The cheapest ticket was for the steerage section. Steerage was at the bottom of the ship. It was not very big, and it had no windows. It was used mostly to carry **cargo,** or boxes and barrels, not people. Even so, hundreds of people packed into the small space. It was uncomfortable. The trip lasted one to three months, depending on the weather.

Once they arrived in America, the immigrants had another challenge. The United States had to accept them. The ships docked at major port cities, like Boston and New York. Here, the immigrants were inspected at immigration centers. The centers wanted to make sure the immigrants didn't have diseases.

Finally, it was time. The immigrants had spent weeks at sea and days at the center. Now it was time to start their new life in the United States.

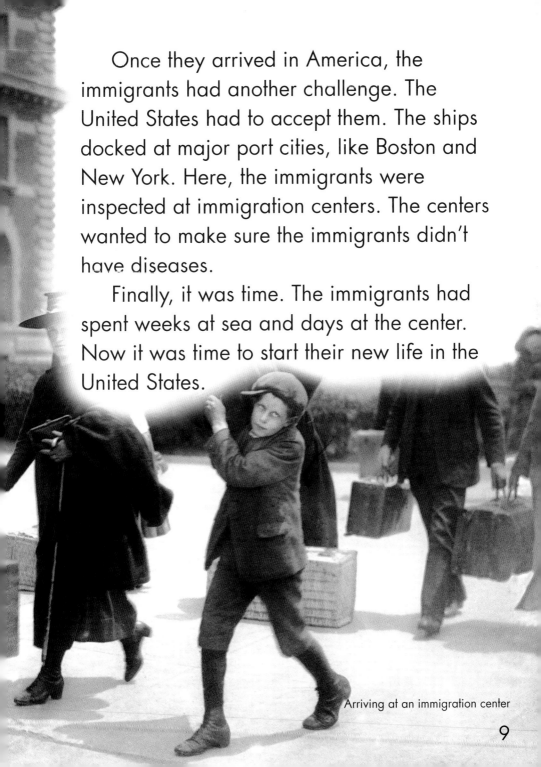

Arriving at an immigration center

Starting Over

For many immigrants, the port city became their new home. Many Irish immigrants settled in Boston. They lived in small apartments and found jobs. At first, America welcomed the hardworking immigrants.

A family hard at work in their kitchen

But the immigrants kept coming. The Potato Famine lasted about ten years. Thousands of families left Ireland. American cities became crowded, and jobs became harder to find. Apartments that once held one family now held four. Shacks were built in backyards and alleys to create additional places for people to live.

Even so, many Irish claimed life was better in the United States than in Ireland. In Ireland, they lived in mud huts. Also, Irish families were sometimes very big. Living in crowded apartments didn't bother them.

The bigger problem was the lack of jobs. Food was plentiful, but it cost money. Without jobs, the families couldn't buy food. Many Irish immigrants were looking for work. With so many workers available, employers could pay the Irish very little money. There was always another immigrant to take the worker's place.

A crowded market in Boston

Not everyone who lived in the U.S. was an immigrant. Some people's families had been in America for many years. Their parents or grandparents might have been immigrants. Many Americans began to worry about all of the immigrants moving into the country. They thought that the immigrants might take their jobs. They worried that the immigrants might have diseases.

People stopped hiring the Irish immigrants. They told the Irish that they didn't have any place for them to live. They told the Irish that they were not welcome. There were simply too many immigrants for the city to handle.

Many Irish immigrants stayed with other people from Ireland. They formed their own neighborhoods in the city. Immigrants from other countries did the same thing. The city began to break up into many separate parts.

The Irish families did not give up. They had worked hard in Ireland. They knew they could work hard in America. They also had an **advantage** over other immigrants. People from Ireland spoke English, not all immigrants did. Immigrants from Italy, for example, spoke Italian. Being able to talk with others who spoke English was very important. It helped the Irish find jobs. It also made them feel more "American."

Even so, Irish families never forgot Ireland. The big city was very different from the Irish countryside. People sometimes call Ireland the Emerald Isle. That's because Ireland has green rolling hills that stretch for miles. There is little green space in the city. Buildings line the streets, and people are everywhere.

The Irish families got used to this, too. They still believed in America's promise of a better life.

A village in Ireland

Getting Ahead

By 1850, one out of every five people in Boston was from Ireland. That's a lot of people! The Irish soon realized that they had power in the city. The government needed them. Unlike in England at that time, Americans **elected** their leaders. Anyone who wanted to lead Boston needed the Irish to vote for them.

Soon the Irish realized that they could do more than vote. They could become a part of the government. They could help lead Boston. As leaders, they could make changes. They could help the Irish immigrants in Boston. They could make a difference for all of Boston's citizens.

Boston

In 1885, a man from Ireland was elected mayor. Hugh O'Brien became the first Irish mayor of Boston.

Hugh had come to America with his parents when he was five years old. When he was 12 years old, he began working for a newspaper. He worked very hard and enjoyed his job. As an adult, he owned his own publishing company.

In 1875, Hugh began to work for the government of Boston. He worked to improve the laws in Boston. He worked to improve the life of Boston's citizens. The people of Boston trusted Hugh. Then he was elected mayor, and he continued to improve the city. He helped set up Boston's parks. He worked to create Boston's public library. He also joined groups to help other people. One group helped orphans, or children without parents. Another group helped Irish immigrants.

Hugh's success was proof that the Irish could succeed in America!

Mayor Hugh O'Brien

19

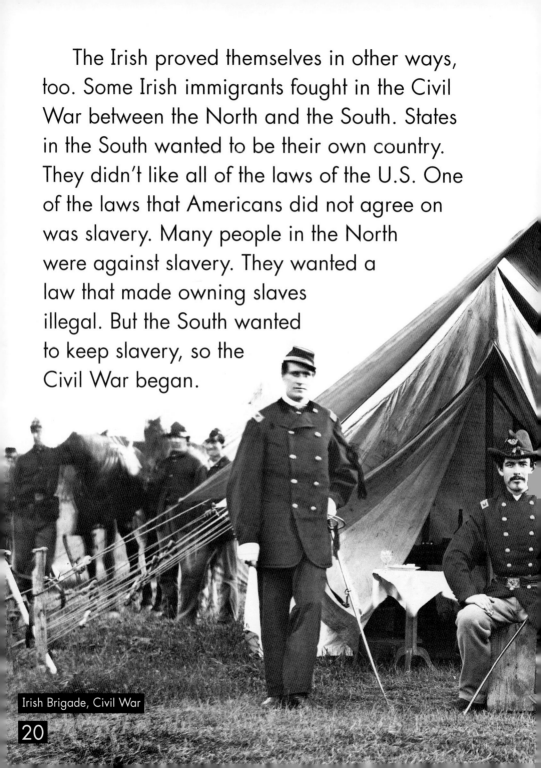

The Irish proved themselves in other ways, too. Some Irish immigrants fought in the Civil War between the North and the South. States in the South wanted to be their own country. They didn't like all of the laws of the U.S. One of the laws that Americans did not agree on was slavery. Many people in the North were against slavery. They wanted a law that made owning slaves illegal. But the South wanted to keep slavery, so the Civil War began.

Irish Brigade, Civil War

Irish immigrants fought for the North. They wanted to prove their loyalty to their new country. They fought bravely. They proved that they were hardworking, loyal people.

Some Irish immigrants also formed labor unions. A labor union is a group that helps workers. Today, work places are watched by the government. Laws tell companies how much to pay people and how to keep them safe.

These laws didn't exist in the 1800s. Some of the most tiring and dangerous jobs were done by Irish immigrants. For example, Irish immigrants helped build the railroad across the United States. They dug canals for waterways. They also mined the mountains for coal.

The companies did not pay the workers very much money. They made them work long hours every day. Some jobs were not healthy, either. So, some Irish immigrants formed labor unions. The labor unions spoke to the companies. They shared their concerns about the workers. They asked for higher pay and safer work places.

Mining coal was a dangerous job.

CHAMPIONS OF AMERICA

Baseball champions in the 1800s

Today, many athletes make a lot of money. People like to watch the athletes play their favorite sports. People buy tickets to watch them play.

In the 1800s, people also liked sports. Some Irish immigrants earned their living as athletes. Some men became boxers. They would fight other people for money. People would pay money to watch the boxing matches. The boxers would then get some of that money.

Baseball also became popular in the 1800s. At first, people just played for fun. Then people began playing for money. People owned the teams, and they paid the players. Playing on a baseball team was another way to earn money. So, many Irish immigrants began playing baseball.

Some Irish immigrants also made changes through writing. As writers, they could express their hopes and concerns. One Irish immigrant writer was a man named John Boyle O'Reilly. He wrote many things, including poems and novels. He was also an editor of a Boston newspaper called *The Pilot*.

Writers like John Boyle O'Reilly paved the way for other Irish writers, like Eugene O'Neill. O'Neill was born in New York in 1888, but his parents were Irish immigrants. He became famous for his plays. He won the Nobel Prize for literature. He won four Pulitzer Prizes for his writing, too. Both are very important awards.

Irish writer Eugene O'Neill

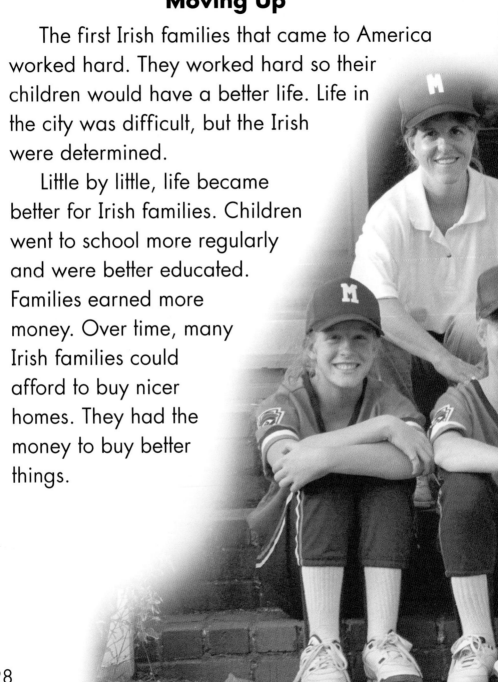

Moving Up

The first Irish families that came to America worked hard. They worked hard so their children would have a better life. Life in the city was difficult, but the Irish were determined.

Little by little, life became better for Irish families. Children went to school more regularly and were better educated. Families earned more money. Over time, many Irish families could afford to buy nicer homes. They had the money to buy better things.

Irish families were no longer just Irish. They were Americans, too. They took a great risk leaving Ireland for a better life in the U.S. The Irish Americans of today can thank their **ancestors** for taking that chance many years ago.

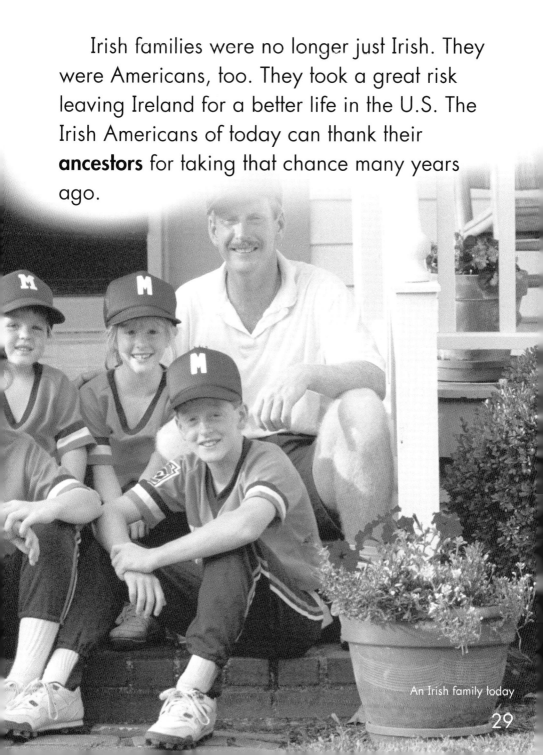

An Irish family today

The Boston Irish Famine Memorial

The Irish immigrants of Boston have not been forgotten. In 1998, a special park was dedicated in their honor. The park has two sculptures and eight plaques. The plaques tell the story of the Irish immigrants. The park is called the Boston Irish Famine **Memorial**.

A man from the Irish government came to the park. He said, "The Memorial will serve as a . . . reminder of the Famine, a story of great loss, but of survival and courage, too."

The Irish immigrants left their homeland of Ireland. But they gained a new home in the United States. They faced many conflicts and problems, but they found ways to solve those problems and have a good life. They made their mark on American history.

The promise of America was fulfilled.

Glossary

advantage: something that helps in getting what is wanted

ancestors: family members born in the past

cargo: the goods carried on a ship, airplane, or vehicle

elected: is chosen by a process of voting

famine: an extreme lack of food

immigrants: people who leave their country to live somewhere else

memorial: something that keeps remembrance alive

rent: payment made for use of something